MOTIVATIONAL
MOMENTS

MOTIVATIONAL

MOMENTS

DONALD L. DOWRIDGE JR.

Visit the author's Web site at
www.dldenterprises.org

Motivational Moments

Copyright © 2018 by Donald L. Dowridge Jr.
All rights reserved. Cover Photo copyright ©
by Anthony Jones. All rights reserved.
Cover Designed by
Anthony Jones & Donald L. Dowridge, Jr.

All rights reserved. Written permission must
be secured from the publisher to use or
reproduce any part of this book, excerpt for
brief quotations in critical reviews or articles.
Published by Tyeroh, Incorporated.
ISBN 978-0-692-10607-5
Library of Congress Catalog Number
First Edition
Printed in the United States

THANK YOU

This book, my fourteenth **(THANK GOD)** is a dedication to the following great people who poured their soul into assuring my perseverance, resilience, success, overcoming, and fulfilling of GOD'S life purpose for myself. These wonderful people felt it not robbery to give their time and knowledge as well a firm hand, as they stood and (Yes) are always still standing by me as a beacon of light and guidance. Though the list is long and there are many people, (too many to list). Definitely you who are not present on this list, you too are forever etched in the fibers of my heart, mind and soul! You like this present list of wonderful people are appreciated. Lastly,

"THANK YOU FOR ALL YOU GAVE TO ME AND I SINCERELY PRAY THAT I HAVE NOT DISAPPOINTED YOU!!!!!!"

MARY ROGERS - ELIZABETH TAYLOR
AUDREY BEST - DARLENE BEST
& THE BEST FAMILY
DONALD L. DOWRIDGE, SR.
DONALD L. DOWRIDGE, III
DONJANAY L. DOWRIDGE
JANICE L. DOWRIDGE- HAYES & FAMILY
JOYCE L. DOWRIDGE & FAMILY
JOHN TAYLOR - FRANKIE McCALL, JR.
MARY CHERRY - ELIZABETH TURNER
ADA STRICKLAND - TRACI COLLINS
FRED BERRY, SR. - VERA SCOTT DORSETT
PASTOR ARTHUR T. JONES
PASTOR WALTER CRAWFORD
PASTOR BARTHOLOMEW BANKS
DAYLE GREENE - EARL DAVIS
OSCAR JOHNSON - MRS. JENNINGS
PAM MORRIS - PAUL BURKE
SHERELL WILSON & ALL THOSE WHO CARED
ENOUGH TO SEE ME THROUGH!

CONTENTS

Dedication	v.
Forward	x.
Acknowledgments	xiii

Motivational Moment Story One	
The Greatest You Holiday	1. & 2.
Motivational Moment Story Two	
Power Up	4.
Motivational Moment Story Three	
T.G.I.F.	6.
Motivational Moment Story Four	
Who Are We?	8.
Motivational Moment Story Five	
I Carry No Frown	10.
Motivational Moment Story Six	
Have You Had Your Love Today?	12.
Motivational Moment Story Seven	
Move By Faith, Not Fear	14.
Motivational Moment Story Eight	
Truth	16.
Motivational Moment Story Nine	
Happy Day	18.
Motivational Moment Story Ten	
Wake Up Everybody	20.
Motivational Moment Story Eleven	
Continue The Dream	22.
Motivational Moment Story Twelve	
Delete Black History	24.
Motivational Moment Story Thirteen	
Standing Ovation	26.
Motivational Moment Story Fourteen	
W.I.N.N.E.R.	28.

Contents

Motivational Moment Story Fifteen	
Are You Great Enough?	30.
Motivational Moment Story Sixteen	
The Sun, Moon & Stars	32.
Motivational Moment Story Seventeen	
F.I.FA.	34.
Motivational Moment Story Eighteen	
What's In Your Closet?	36.
Motivational Moment Story Nineteen	
Ring, Ring Go The Bell	38.
Motivational Moment Story Twenty	
Finding Favor	40.
Motivational Moment Story Twenty-One	
Thanks – Giving	42.
Motivational Moment Story Twenty-Two	
10	44.
Motivational Moment Story Twenty-Three	
In With The New	46.
Motivational Moment Story Twenty-Four	
Our Achievements	48.
Motivational Moment Story Twenty-Five	
A Man	50.
Motivational Moment Story Twenty-Six	
Great	52.
Motivational Moment Story Twenty- Seven	
Will Overcome	54.
Motivational Moment Story Twenty-Eight	
Don't Want Nobody	56.
Motivational Moment Story Twenty-Nine	
Get It, Get It!	58.
Motivational Moment Story Thirty	
Done	60.
Motivational Moment Story Thirty-One	
Best Love	62.

Contents

THE CONCLUSION
Retrospect   **64.**
DLD Offerings
Previous Books
THANK YOU

FORWARD

Here you are cruising into the moments. These could be the most important moments of your life. Moments that may spur you ahead in your aspiration of succeeding forward to your mark of greatness.

This could be the moment why you decided to purchase this book. Within this book can be the ticket awaiting your arrival to the next door to your elevation! As the author I *thank you* in advance for taking the time to invest in this book. Ahead is *thirty - one* moments recorded over the years beginning in two thousand - seven. These moments were featured in nation's newspapers, radio programs & online. These moments have been medicine for many. This is a sworn admission; *these moments have also assisted me in my journey as well.* We all go through a crisis in our lifetime. Some come through those crises, unfortunately some don't prevail, *they sink*!!!!! *Where are you at this point in your life?*

Knowing this is not your situation, however if it is you, this is the moment designed especially for you. This is the wakeup call, new beginnings of your new destiny. Taking you on a zooming ride like you have never experience before in your life. This is a golden opportunity, if not already elevated into the life you seek. *The life you seek is awaiting you!* How long will you take? Fortunately, you have a chance, and *this is your chance.* Take this moment and believe you can *fly as if a spanking new eagle!*

This is it! Again
"THIS IS IT, STOP WASTING PRECIOUS TIME!!"

Motivational Moments is the name of this book. It is the *Motivational Moments* that I had to suff er through. It is the *Motivational Moments* that I prevail through. With the gracious love of *"JESUS CHRIST"* these *Motivational Moments* became my helpmate and Honestly, *"I AM SOO HAPPY FOR THESE MOTIVATIONAL MOMENTS AND TO SHARE THEM WITH YOU!"*

These *Motivational Moments*, if allowed will serve you in the same manner as myself. *If read, if believed, if inserted in your long-term memory, your heart, the fiber of your soul,* surely, you'll be elevated beyond the norm of just living a everyday normal life. Question: *Why just live a normal life?* Expand beyond the norm, you were born with an extraordinary flame of agility.

When you were born the world stopped and gave you a Standing Ovation. That's right, a *"STANDING OVATION!"* You were born with Special Gifts and Talents! "Allow these *Motivational Moments* to assist you in the discovery of the *New You*!!"

These *Motivational Moments* are about the *Greatest You Holiday*, how to *Power Up, T.G.I.F., I Carry No Frown, Had You Have Your Love Today, WINNER, Will Overcome, Oh Happy Day, Are You Great Enough, Get It, Get It and Done!*

It is truly a blessing to be able to write these stories from my heart for many people who are eyeing their internal & external greatness.

In life we all need that extra boost! As my mentor Mr. Les Brown states, *"LIFE HAPPENS"* and you must grow through it in order to reach your goals and success. Know this, there are no way out of this life alive. We all must die, why not die on empty, why not give your all every single day of your life? Life is a joy, why not, why not live it to the fullest until that last day!

Motivational Moments is here, and it is ready to take you directly to your dream. If these moments are heartfelt try and place them directly within you.

Like the late great comedian Richard Pryor would say in his act as Mudball, *"GRAB THAT SUN AND RUB IT ALL OVER YOU AND YOU BE THE SUN RAYS IN YOUR LIFE AND SOMEBODY ELSES LIFE."* Somebody needs your *"Sunrays"* so why not ***"SHINE!"***

In closing I Thank You for spending your hard earn currency to purchase this book. This book, *"MOTIVATIONAL MOMENTS"* is not a regret purchase. It's a purchase of satisfaction and I wish you marvelous success and a new journey of living a wonderful, happy, joyful life.

Live "U" to the fullest!

THANK YOU VERY MUCH AND GOD BLESS YOU!!!!!

Donald L. Dowridge, Jr.
Author
Motivational Moments

ACKNOWLEDGEMENT
By
Earl Davis, Jr.
2002 Winter Olympic Torchbearer and CEO,
Create Winners International

Most people like success stories. Do you?

If moments are fleeting, memories are permanent. We share our most powerful memories so that they grow with time rather than fade, giving us the ability to celebrate.

I believe that life is not measured by the number of breaths we take, but by the moments that take our breath away.

Every once in a while, life concedes an elusive moment; it loosens its possessive grip on time, and lets you sink inextricably into beauty of the now, with neither pull from the past, nor allure of the future. These are the moments of pure contented elation, extraordinary in their simplicity. These are moments that tattoo themselves to your soul so that by the time you have the wisdom to reflect back on your life, a significant part of you is a patchwork of these snippets in time. Pristine snapshots, mere glimmers in the long light of your life, but they are unforgettable, unshakeable, in – extinguishable glimmers.

You will probably only get a handful of these transcendent moments in your life. Time will seem to stand still, and nothing but the authenticity of the moment you're in will matter; it is the feeling of complete uninhibited, liberated happiness. It's a visceral feeling, uncomplicated and never in need of validation or explanation. You know it when it hits you. There is no way to not know.

It's usually something simple. It's why people crave watching a sunset while sitting by your local river walk or on a hill in the French countryside, with nothing but a loved one, a bottle of wine, some cheese and some freshly picked strawberries, along with endearing, romantic conversation. It washes over you, and fills you up. You wish nothing more than to bottle it and keep it forever, stealing a small sip each night so you never forget what it means to be unequivocally fulfilled by your own existence. But somehow, you know that part of what makes it so special, is the fact that it's limited. If it were a feeling you had always, it might lose its magic, or, more likely, it would become worn down and beleaguered by the endless avalanche of life's inherent complications.

In late October 2006, my whole world rearranged itself after hearing the words: MOM'S GOT CANCER! I was told by her doctors that she had only two weeks to live and to start preparing family. I'll never forget that moment. How do you motivate yourself to tell someone that? Especially, someone you love!

I didn't tell my mother what the doctors had said until a year and a half later when she felt within herself that she could move mountains. She ultimately passed in her sleep six years later, with a smile on her face. Although there were lots of happy, motivating, encouraging moments during that time when she died, something changed within me. I didn't feel like doing the things that I loved anymore. The successful business that I had built didn't hold the same joy or meaning. Worst of all, I had lost confidence in myself. I knew what I had to do, but for some reason I simply did not do what I knew I had to do. I later learned that what I was experiencing was grief and I was searching for meaning. My personal battle between 2012 and 2015 was to gain power over my own thoughts. To regain power over my thoughts, I began reading and listening to great thoughts from great people…and then made those thoughts mine. Slowly but surely, my personal and professional life began to turn, and I began to win again.

Donald L. Dowridge, Jr. is one of the great men that I continue to learn from, and hold close his words of motivation and wisdom. His performance mastery and knowledge of Frederick Douglass is admirable.

One of the benefits of working with Donald is observing him in action in real life. Observing how he's dealt with difficult times and how he's learned to extract the healing elixir from the power contained in a moment. Over the years, I have gotten to know Donald, as well as the "speaker / celebrity Donald." I have found that he is one in the same person, the genuine article… In fact, he is actually bigger in real life than his celebrity.

It is amongst the highest of honors to be asked to write the Foreword for this book, *Motivational Moments,* because teaching me to capture, learn, and savor the moments in life has not only been motivational but also rewarding. Donald taught me to give every day the chance to become the most beautiful day of your life. The most rewarding thing in life is the patience to wait for the right moment. This is the gift that Donald has given my family and me …a gift he shares with the world…a gift more valuable than money.

While part of us will always wish for the best moments to last forever, we know, ultimately, that they neither can nor should. We know that part of what reveals them as perfect, part of what imbues them with their unique magnificence, is their very juxtaposition to everything else: all the rest of the world's imperfections. Only in proximity to the storm's relentless turbulence, can we see most clearly, the serenity in the calm. Without the storm, we might confuse the calm for mundane; we might fail to recognize the exceptional in the ordinary, the sublime in the simple. So, it is the very fleetingness of these moments that alerts us to their existence; the irony is that if they were always there, we might never recognize their presence.

Every moment has its place, and every moment passes, there is both beauty and comfort in that truth. You can endure the different moments because you know they will not last forever.
And you should soak up the perfect ones, for exactly the same reason.

Finally, to quote Will Smith in the movie HITCH: "Never lie, steal, cheat, or drink. But if you must lie, lie in the arms of the one you love. If you must steal, steal away from bad company. If you must cheat, cheat death. And if you must drink, drink in the moments that take your breath away."

This book is definitely one of those moments and I wish you Godspeed on your journey. Ready. Set. "WIN!"

NOTES

1 THE GREATEST YOU HOLIDAY

How fortunate are we to be able to arise each day? How fortunate are we to be able to enjoy life as we do? Just two questions I poise to those who which to validate a complaint. No, I am not turning a blind eye to the current state of America and to the current state of our great country. I can't help but to see, feel and be a part of the plight that is hovering over this nation. But I must recognize this fact, we are alive! *Yes, we are alive!* This statement is pointed at those blessed to be reading these words at this moment.

I recently read 2nd Timothy 1:7; it struck me when my eyes laid upon this; *"for God has not given us the spirit of fear; but of power, and love and of a sound mind."* It got me to think, if we could just tune into the no fear, the power, and the sound mind, imagine what the outcome will lead to. Because the plight of economics is prevalent, that does not mean it is a time to hand out tickets to the "Quit Concert." That's right the **"Quit Concert!"**

Recognize how great you are and what you must bring to the table. First, we know God don't make junk! Second, if it's not known, then it is now, on the day we were born, *"The World Stopped and Gave Us a Standing Ovation!"* Recognize each time you look at the person in the mirror, you are taking an eyeshot of you, Number "1!"

The Greatest You!

THE END

2 YOUR HOLIDAY

In your lifetime, how many blessings have you survived? How many have you *taken advantage of?*

Those questions lead me to the topic of this story.

"The Greatest You Holiday."

Each new day God give to you, handle it with extreme care.

Know that within the day, there will be hurdles to cross and tough decisions to be made. All in all, continue forth with the notion that you are, and you come from *"Greatness."* Also bear in mind that you have been awarded another chance. So, on your holiday, go on and perform your dance. It's okay if you are the only one that see it fit to perform. *The Greatest You Holiday* is that chance to stand on the platform afforded you by the one and only. Don't be shy to display your joy and happiness.

Hopefully it will spur others in your circle and life to join in and get their *"Greatest You Holiday"* on. For those who wish to condemn and find fault, let them! It will be them who are allowing doubt to stop them from acknowledging how great they truly are. The Spinners once sing, *"It's A Shame"* and I agree.

So, reader, this new day afforded you, get up, get involved, and get into your abilities to administer something awesome from you. Share and spread what we as a people really need to know right about now, that it is a holiday, what holiday?

"THE GREATEST YOU HOLIDAY!"

Now go on and celebrate with no regret. It's your party, now go and enjoy what you deserve! From me to you, from this day forth, it will be your holiday, enjoy and please take *goooood* care of it.

"Hands that help are Hands that care."

THE END

3 POWER UP

Let me begin with this truth, we are living in one of the greatest times known to mankind. We've embarked on history making events. Our eyes have witness, as we embarked on situations that for some have left them in distinct awe. So now is the season to prepare yourself to not be left on the sideline of history.

It is written clear as day in the book of Ecclesiastes Chapter 3 vs. 3. At the end of that verse, it states, *"and a time to build up."* It doesn't get any simpler than that! As a Motivational Guru, one of my main purposes is to encourage and to enhance as I go through. To indulge many in seeing how much greater they are as oppose to what they claim not to be. No, everyone will not lay their weapons of hate, bigotry, prejudice, pain, drugs, alcohol, misery, racism and guns down, but I assure you that a seed of hope will be planted within. It is hoped one will salvage their awaiting greatness.

R.A.K.E., seeing this word brings to your mind a vision of someone out in the yard gathering leaves in the autumn breeze. Hold up, scratch that vision with the quickness! In this content is a method that will surely expose your joy and bring overwhelming happiness. I challenge you to daily live in a position that you will commit a **R**andom **A**ct of **K**indness with **E**nthusiasm*!*

Give this a good thought; people you are kind to, and people who you are enthused about will be powered up at your conscious concern for them. A concern that does not consist of a hidden agenda (*what's in it for me*). *Just Do It*! Like MasterCard, (*Priceless*)!

In a recent reading, there was a paragraph that would add meaning to the phrase, "POWER UP!" *"As long as our sole focus is on financial gain and greed, we will surely miss out on the true luxuries of life that are priceless!"*

If you can honestly gear your heart to *"POWER UP"* another as you go through life, you will activate a situation of favor on your behalf. After reading this, I was compelled to think how true to life this is.

Each of us have the answer to a successful life installed within. We all come equipped with our own joy and happiness intact. Unfortunately some of us fall weak and are in need of that brave someone to make a guest appearance and *power us up*. To unleash some *love, compassion, understanding, and some "yes you can."* Are you this person?

From this day forth make a promise to yourself that you will **"R.A.K.E."** and **"Power Up"** someone on a daily basis. *You surely will not regret it, you will only benefit from it!*

THE END

4   **T.G. I. F.**

Over the years I have learned a lot about my self being. Hopefully you the reader have gained in-depth knowledge about yourself over the years as well. Isn't it just amazing how our human mind conceives what we hear and what we see?

How many times in the midst of receiving information, we found it not to be what we thought we heard? In other words, your mind decides to deceive you (lol). Somehow, we can receive our own thoughts on what word, sentence and or action means to our personal self. For instance, you may relate a certain phrase to an event or something that might have accrued in your past. Likewise, you might attempt to think in the same fashion with a spoken word. Each time you hear it spoken, right away it may take you directly to that moment in your life. It sends a spark to your mental bank which in turn send a message to your active self which may bring about memories of a time gone by in your life. How many of you are able to put this paragraph in proper perspective? *Hmmmmmmmm!!*

Forthcoming is a perfect example of this motivational moment in print. I mention "T.G.I.F." and automatically you think of a famous restaurant or in the sense of working an eight to five with weekends off !

"Thank God It's Friday!"
I'm living for the weekend!!!!

Now let's look at the same acronym from another angle. "**T**ake **G**reat **I**nitiative with **F**ulfillment."

Think on this phrase for a second. Now say it a few times to your inner self, now repeat it out loud. What do you think?

Motivational Moments

In every aspect of your life be consistent in taking great initiative to apply faith with a positive mental attitude which will allow for going the extra mile. Set your mind to seeing the vision of your total success which, should split the sea of doubt and lead you across the rivers of achievement. As Smokey The Bear once said, *"Only you can prevent forest fires!"* Your success lies on how bad you want it and how much it means to you in achieving it.

"**T**. **G**. **I**. **F**." in this content bring to mind great people like, *Cullen Jones* (Olympic swimmer), *Tiron Wise* (Valedictorian), *Tamara Shamburger* (Hillsborough County School Board), *Brandi Ahonsi* (Formerly of Life Link of Florida), *Cathy Hughes* (Radio One, Inc. Founder), *David Ruiz* (Graduate), *Candy Lowe* (Black Business Bus Tour), *Corey Felton* (King Cobra Enterprises), *Oliver Crawford* (S.I.N.G. Productions) and finally rounding out this list of individuals who are **T**aking **G**reat **I**nitiative with **F**ulfillment, *Howard Smith* (Program Director, HBI). There is a must to recognize as well, *Mr. Chuck Taylor* (who guided me to receiving a college degree). Most of these people can be found paving a path for many, one way or another. Majority listed above are happy residence of the "Soul of the Bay," better known to the world as: "T-A-M-P-A," Florida.

Everyday can be **"T.G.I.F,"** just make that commitment to be the best "**U**" at all times and live with true commitment and with a knack to live it to your fulfillment. It's **"T.G.I.F.!"** Are you willing to ***"T.G.I.F?"***

THE END

4   WHO ARE WE

A mere four hundred years, a mere four hundred years of achievements, a mere four hundred years of inventions, and a mere four hundred years of investments. What does four hundred years have to do with the current state of our status today?

It has a lot to do with it!

It has a lot to do with our youth for the most part. It also has a lot to do with our adults, as well as our elders who have fought so hard opening doors, so we can enjoy our existence today in a lap of luxury. That's right, in case you didn't read that last sentence right or if it didn't register. I'll repeat, we are living in the lap of our elders and ancestors. ***We are living today in a lap of luxury they fought for!!***

Do we really know who we are and the importance of our being? In Dennis Kimbro's book entitled, "Daily Motivations for African – American Success," he states, *"We are Achievers, and we are doctors, lawyers, writers, and entrepreneurs. We are visionaries, innovators, dreamers, creators, leaders, builders, and doers. We are survivors, over comers, and we know the meaning of perseverance. We have carved out a slate of history by standing strong in the midst of turbulence. Many before us made great strides so we can forgo a painful existence!"*

Who are we? Dating back way before those famous ships started heading towards these American shores, it is recorded that we were shareowners, not sharecroppers. We stood tall as warriors and we took extreme care of our own. We were described as proud and most definitely we protected our own. We utilized hard work, self- confidence, and unshakable faith.

Motivational Moments

"UNSHAKABLE FAITH!"

I say, *Who are we?*
    In these days and times unfortunately, we deal with a media system that elevates a taste of gloom. A media that want us to believe what is wrong somehow is right. What's going on here, we have and will defy the odds. As Elton John once said, *"We are still standing"* and we are steadily moving on up with no intentions of stopping now. We look back to travel forth into conquering dreams of prosperity. We have been delegated to carry the torch that was handed to us from great people of our past. The majority of our people who made a name for themselves did not come with a golden spoon. They came from homes and an area of town that was considered poor and destitute, however they emerged as stars.

    Hold on, wait a dog-gone minute; we are *Dr. Ben Carson, Lisa Leslie, Julian Bond, Harry Belafonte, Barack & Michele Obama, Billie Holiday, Fred Shuttlesworth, Quincy Jones, Otis Anthony, Mary Cherry, Rosa Parks, Mr. & Mrs. Richard Love, Michele Patty, C. Blythe Andrews, Pastor Bart Banks, Doreatha Edgecombe, W.E.B. Dubois, Warren Dawson, Dr. Rosemary Johnson, The Late Pastor Arthur T. Jones, Pastor Donald White & First Lady Marie T. White, Jesse Williams, Lorenzo Myles & Mr. Otis Williams (who is still carrying The Temptations)!*

    This is just a small crop of African Americans today and yesterday who pushed, and still are pushing the envelope to help keep us in the right direction of *hope, productivity,* and *success.* It's not who we are, it's we are:

"ACHIEVERS!"

!!! THAT'S WHO WE ARE!!!

THE END

5   I CARRY NO FROWN

"I do not cry, I will not cry, Period!"

    Documentation has provided a universal paper-trial flatly showing evidence of an African-American people realizing their value and worth here in America. We know the hardships that we have faced through the years. As if an Olympic runner who must jump over each and every hurdle, we have ran and jumped many to land on successful ground for which we stand today. In our running and jumping these hurdles, we have gone on to accomplish great feats that we all as a race can be very proud and exhilarated about.

Stand Proud!

"We are on the Winners Platform!"

    There will be no bashing from this motivated writer; however, what you will get instead is a hearty dose of how we persevered and engineered our way past the many who demonstrated in a distained manner at our optimistic character and demeanor. Rapper and actor, LL Cool J in his song, *"Mama said knock you out"* gave us a line that stated, *"don't call it a setback, call it a comeback!"* African-American setbacks for the large part truly has equated to a setup. You know the deal, *"a setback is a setup to success."* There is not enough space here to expound on the trials that we suffered due to our petitioning to be accepted as equal. Here we stand on a solid ground that afford us the availability to continue to chaperon each new generation toward *greater intelligence, views, respect, choices, and professionalism.* To rekindle whatever expiring embers of confidence that is attempting to flee.

"I CARRY NO FROWN!"

There is no sign of blindness and I am well acquainted to the pitfalls, issues, turmoil and division that we are currently suffering through. I bypass these ills to focus on the brighter side of darkness. So as to commend us who repeatedly soak ourselves in the gratification of our ongoing determination, resurrection and glorious triumphs. We know as our elders know, *"and this too shall pass."* The passing of time has certainly opened the doors for us too!!!

"AND STILL I RISE!!"

"Stand Proud, Focus, Heart and Mind!"

If there may be any dismalness, wipe it away now. *There is no need to frown.* There is no need to cry. Though, if there is a reason to tear, let it be from joy, let it be from the dispersing of many acknowledged victories that we lay acclaim to and or is associated with. The past we derived from have surely set us up for our victories of this present time. So, captivate an attitude of defiance and assurance with your every wakening hour. Comb through the barrage of destructive pleasantries. Forge forth with a spirit and desire to add your spice of newness and determination to a life purpose. **I Carry No Frown** and I can only hope that you too won't carry a frown, instead of a frown, how about a *"SMILE!"*

You too can tell the stories of the days that got us here and will continue to take us where the victories lie awaiting the presence of us!

THE END

Motivational Moments

6 HAVE YOU HAD YOUR LOVE TODAY?

The Mighty O'Jays in the late 1970's asked this question, *"Have You Had Your Love Today?"* Seem like a very simple question that equates to the subject of L-O-V-E.

My dear friend we all must admit to the fact that it is really true, *love make the world go around.* Then *gee wheeze, Batman,* what's up with all this hate? It's like there is a grocery store centrally located in every town of America with isles inside similar to a regular grocery store. Publix, Giants, Safe Way, Super Fresh & Winn Dixie come to mind. However, there is one diff erence to these stores, there is *"HATE!"* I know hate is a strong word, however a scope of reality must be presented. There are people just like you and I who daily visit these type stores and *shop for "hate of the day."* Once they are finished shopping, they then *spend their day spitting this hate everywhere and on everybody!* Did I say **"EVERYBODY?"**

Love is in the air and everyday it is traveling, circulating throughout you & me. We know or we should know that each day we are allowed to awaken; we should awaken with some sense of love in place. Going back to when God himself gave love, he gave love by giving of himself so that we, his children who are made in his image would likewise demonstrate that same type of love to each other. It's simple math here, we are born into a family that we have no control of. Saying that, hopefully if not the environment we are born in, then just maybe the family we are born in will give, nurture and adorn that baby with an abundance of love. In return the genuine love given to that off spring will flourish to a point where this baby will grow and likewise want to double his/her love of self and others within this entire world.

Poet Maya Angelou said it best, *"My great hope is to laugh as much as I cry; to get my work done and try to love somebody and have the courage to accept the love in return."*

As you read this piece, I pray you walk away and let these words melt into your every being and (as crazy as it sounds) step to someone and just let them know how much love you have for them. In return you might, I say might just make their day and just might be unknowingly changing somebody's miserable day. Showing love mean that you might just be saving a life.

I've found just within myself how much love I have to go around. The key to my love success is I had to learn to love myself first and then I could love everybody else. In conclusion, the question still come to this; **"Have You Had Your Love Today?"**

Just knowing you have love makes a world of difference in your demeanor. It also plays a huge part in how you show real love to *your spouse, your family, friends, companion, associates, coworkers, and even, strangers.*

Here's my plead, we already know how tough it is these days, but if we can manage to love self a little more, we can *love others even greater.* I challenge us to just try to love each other just a little more. *Try it, guarantee you will love it!*

THE END

7   MOVE BY FAITH, NOT FEAR

"Hebrew Chapter 11 vs. 7 states by faith Noah, being warned of God of things not seen as yet, moved by fear, prepared an ark to the saving of his house."

How many of us are legitimately and unequivocally not moved to act until some type of fear is set in motion? Well I'm pretty sure we all have experienced being tee-tee afraid to move forward in our desires. Oh yea, we've even talked a good game about what we are going to do, and because of fear, we talked ourselves out of bringing our best foot forward. Some over the years have figured, *"what the heck, I'll bamboozle my way through, or I'll act my way through."* In the end they were the one, *"bamboozled."*

These days many pellets have been tossed towards the glass ceilings of desire. The results of all those pellets over the years has resulted into 18 million cracks in the glass ceiling of desire. With that comes no excuse to choke up and throw the white towel of surrender. It's no marginal mirage that we are a part of this door opening horizon. As the new morning awakens the breath of sunshine within you, have the courage, courage to grab hold of that miserable tyrant called fear and force fear, *I said it!* Force fear to recognize that it will not detour you from accomplishing your feat of victory.

Step up to the plate, use initiative as your bat, hit with faith. The rewards that you will be entitled to will be just the ignition needed to propel you in the direction you wish to travel. Aw! The power of moving by faith; So what you can't feel it, you can't see it, but God know if you stay true to the "faith" and continue to press forward, you will further garnish great jubilation despite the judgmental attitude of the disavowed.

Motivational Moments

In your own little corner of your world be subtle in your progression. Faith; be like the Easter Bunny and the Rocket Scientist having something in common, now that is *"Unbelievable!"* They might not have the nerve to believe in you. Do you have the nerve to take it up a notch and caress the engine of hope and drive faith straight to the highest height?

Wherever you may rise, shake the notion of fear and impregnate yourself with a force-field that won't shackle you like a thieve about to make off with the prize of your life.

Shelter the goodness and stretch what is aching to expand from your lions. It's all good and all in motion, just step in the name of what will become a known fact about you, *"you took the leap of faith!"* The end result will be infused with integrity and your will to struggle through it all.

Who said it was supposed to be a smooooth ride to the end? Oh noooo, life is a test of all our strength. I do feel sorry for all of my brothers and sisters who awaken just to go right back to sleep. This do not describe you even in the remote of the sense of what is meant by *faith, faith, faith!*

I hear many say they are worried about their job, their home, their whatever. One thing I have learned, *"It's Faith!"* There are trillions of distractions, like a billboard seeking to capture the psyche. Once it gets you, you are gotten! The end of all ends is to:

"MOVE BY FAITH, NOT FEAR!"

THE END

8   **TRUTH**

    Words in Webster Dictionary give in some instance a variety of meanings for one word. In my case, I gather an abundance of word meanings so as to give clarity and precise understanding of the word I'm seeking to use or speak with. There is no exception for the word we all know as "Truth." It is in these stories the main line and it is what will be brought to light. Just for edification purpose and to be exact in the contents of this piece I called on Mr. Webster. Let's see what Mr. Webster has to give us under the word Truth. *"The state of being Truthful, and Honesty!"* Now this is the real deal!

    Truth is known in the heart, accepted in the mind, and should be enacted daily in our life. It's called, owning up to the truth. In a famous movie of a few years gone by, Jack Nickolas uttered the memorable line, *"You can't handle the truth!"* God we all know the truth will set us free and likewise we know telling the truth release us from stress related issues that can and will become a strain on the brain and more importantly a dreaded health crisis. Let go and let loose for it will save face and later embarrassment of the fifth power, *"oh that hurts!"*

    Don't become or don't be a victim of what is called *"Truth Leasing!"* This phase is derived from when a person is so adapted to fibbing, they try to come up with a false truth to cover the lie they just got busted telling. So, in the end they attempt what I call, *"Truth Leasing!"* Simply put, leasing the truth. Some of us are so oblivious to the truth that it would surely cause hospital stay for telling the truth.

    Thank God for those who are keen to discernment. Aunt Esther was quick to tell Fred Sanford, *"Watch it Sucker!"* When there is discernment in place, how far does a lie travel before it is shut down and sent packing?

A lie instead of the truth can be as deadly as hurricane Gustav hitting the gulf coast, "DEADLY!" Let's talk about the truth and nothing but the whole truth. Why go out your way to tell a lie when the truth will set you free? *Is it because the real truth hurt?* I like how Mark Twain (*1835 – 1910*) describes the truth by saying, *"if you tell the truth, you don't have to remember anything."* How revealing is that when we can save our brain and our memory bank from mustering up a fable that will only be axed. Leaving the perpetrator to savor in their own detention because of regretting a lie told.

In whatever you truly decide to make of your life or whatever you might have championed in your life, whether you are a novice in your walk or a seasoned veteran with a wealth of experience under your belt, practice and continue to exercise being a person of valor and truth. Let honor and truth mark you as you confront situations that may pose a threat to what you stand for. Grow in truth for that will be the bouquet discharging an essence of self-respect. This too will open a relationship of favor with your peers and others alike.

In final thoughts, let this marinade in your LTM *(Long Term Memory),* Truth is the defining line of what is expected of self. A lie will only alienate you from everybody else. *Think about it!*

THE END

9   OH HAPPY DAY!

    Don't even begin to illiterate to anyone how much of a distorted day you are having! It could be a day that consists of a short fuse thereby bringing on negative consequences. It also can be a day others will deliver an orgy of ignorance to your doorstep. Lastly, it can be a day that your happiness is jolly-stomped. We all have had the misty eyes in the middle of a terrible thunderstorm, tornado, and earthquake.
Plain and simple, *we have all had our world rocked!*

    As you might agree those types of days are not the best of best days. *"Doctor, doctor what do you have for a migraine headache?"* How many of you reading this piece can honesty proclaim there is some familiarity in this situation? Not many can truthfully come forth and draw attention to this fact. Let the truth be known, life has a way of evaporating the world of *"Peaches & Cream, no matter how great it may seem."*

    And the choir sing:
"Oh Happy Day!" "Oh Happy Day!" "Oh Happy Day!"

    These are powerful words that must be adorned like a suit of armor meant to ward off naysayers with animosity. It is the suit of armor that is capable of keeping at bay the pessimistic that bask in your down spiral. They have a grand agenda aimed at your flopping. Their only purpose is to put you in an unwanted dilemma. To stop you dead in your tracks!

    OH HAPPY DAY is here and celebration is in order so wipe the blur of despair from your vision. Celebrate yourself, be your greatest cheerleader. Find *JOY* and *HAPPYINESS*; be proud enough to keep it with you every step of the way in your life.

Motivational Moments

OH HAPPY DAY is not getting caught up in doubting what you are born to produce. Some allow themselves to get lost in the sauce that drowns out their loudest desires of accomplishment.

OH HAPPY DAY is having a mission to carry forth and rewarding self as the mission is completed. Don't dwell on the issue that it might fail. Many have failed their way to success just by staying focus.

OH HAPPY DAY is to honor your abilities and recognize what others may not want to recognize, *"U'R MAGNIFICENT!"* You are a walking glow of *"AUGUST!"* That turns out to be an accomplishment within its own right.

OH HAPPY DAY is to take time out of your hectic schedule and *"HANG WITH SUPPORTERS."* Exchanging dialogue that will eventually expose you to your next highlight. Take the road less adorned, it will steer you clear of worrywarts.

Brave the *"Storms of Doubt," "Slothfulness of Animosity,"* & *"Boom of Failure."* Just be a *"Baller!"* Roll high stakes in *"Celebrating You," "Happiness in Your Abilities,"* & *"Hanging with Supporters!"* A new sun is a joyful day; A new blessing is ***"OH HAPPY DAY!"***

THE END

10   WAKE UP EVERYBODY

    Family and friends, we are about to pull up to the bumper of another Christmas Holiday. This is the season to be jolly, it's also the season that ring in awareness of what should be a better and exciting year ahead. It is the cognizance of a new era vastly dawning upon us (*ready or not you can't hide; it's going to find you*). Now the only way one won't be found is to be *vacant, ghost, coma, dead,* or like in a *forever sleep zone*. If you are reading this piece well… So, with the grace of our Lord and Savior, you too will be making the pilgrimage into the coming year of Two Thousand and Twenty.

    As we the people of color advance into the New Year, let us hold our horses and act today on this holiday season. This is the next to last big holiday of these decades. Next year mark twenty years, which began in the year 2010 and concludes in this year of 2019.

    In standing at the threshold of this Christmas joy, take a moment to soak up the *LOVE GOD* has supplied us with along with what he has allowed us to experience within these two decades. You will apply to be in agreement when it is mentioned how far we have come and how much we have experience. It is written in *Ecclesiastes Chapter 3* about *the time of our life.* I'm sure somewhere in these two decades *someone lost a special person, someone gained a companion, someone enjoyed a wonderful laugh of meaning, someone was inspired by powerful words or a good novel, someone gave us understanding of our undertakings, someone witness a new birth, someone became an entrepreneur and someone gave their life to Christ.*

    With all that engaging news we should be energized to delete any signs of procrastination which might cause one to have an inconvenient appointment within the next year.

Motivational Moments

Use this holiday season to enjoy the essence of family and friends. Use this season also to reflect on what was and what is to be in your future. Be incredible and decisive as you bring alertness to those who will attempt to use each given day to be slothful and incontinence. Knowing tomorrow is not promise to us should be the marking to act today on great possibilities. Use every minute to hone in on your off erings to the world at large.

"Wake Up Everybody No More Procrastination" as two thousand and nineteen begin to take its rightful place. Be prepared to take advantage of the opportunities coming, be aplomb to receive opportunities as they knock. Bring your "A" game, it will assure *"if I Woulda, Shoulda, Coulda done that"* won't stop by for coff ee. I can share stories of those coff ee breaks *(a charade of the worst kind)*.

Last words: Let Two Thousand and Nineteen chronicle your great accomplishments with no procrastination!

Merry Christmas, Happy Kwanzaa, Happy Hanukkah
&
Happy New Years To Y-O-U!

PEACE

THE END

11   CONTINUE THE DREAM

"**I am proud that God is a God that answers prayers.**" The preacher told the congregation on a very important day in December of 1956, while history was being made. The preacher went on to tell the parishioners, *"starting Monday we will be going back to the buses."*

That was the result of a unity effort within a people following the *"Dreamer"* who believed in freedom. A *"Dreamer"* who had unseen faith that one day the sealed doors of freedom would open. A people of diverse cultures knew hatred was putting a freeze on life as it could be; they were ready for the chains to be released. Spreading like wildfire of togetherness, claiming small victories and triumphs as they clocked into another day of discrimination and bigotry. The victories which would take its toll on those lined with a mansion of hate, tearing at their fiber with marches, sit-ins, rallies, and of course a whole lot of praying to our God.

By maintaining grace and belief in non-violence, hate as huge as Mount Saint Helen's was evidently moved. Though the pain suffered was of huge proportions, a people managed to triumph.

Here we are just over sixty-three years removed from the era of the Montgomery bus boycott and the victory that ensued as a result of *persistence, perseverance, prayer and peace.*

As an elder who was born during those turbulent fifties and sixties, there is assurance of hate, stinging those hard-fought victories that led a people of color and people of the world to draw strength from. It is known that the elders of today *(the majority of them)* stayed the course of the *"Dreamer."*

Those of us who were in our *diapers, riding our tricycles,* or just starting *our first years of school,* for the most part we had no idea of what season we were living. Maybe that is why we are called *the children of the sixties, you think?*

Even though the *"Dreamer"* was taken from us on that fatal night of *April Fourth, Nineteen Sixty-Eight,* we must always keep in mind, what he started is on our shoulders to continue.

As our children of the twenty-first century, begin to take their rightful place in this new America, it is surely being found that many people of color are very displeased at some of the negative that has sprung loose; *and it is loose!*

Keep in mind, continuing the *"Dreamers"* dream should be the vehicle of our joy in passing the torch on. *Always claim the victory even in a setback. Know that in every life some rain must fall. Understand the righteous will prevail over the evildoer. We were born to dream, just act on those dreams for they just might be a major invention to saving the world.*

CELEBRATING YOU

"REV. DR. MARTIN LUTHER KING, JR."

THE END

12 DELETE BLACK HISTORY

Few years ago, 2007 to be exact there was a news story centered around the remarks made by "Lean On Me" lead actor Mr. Morgan Freeman. Being an African-American History Pack-Rat, in my archives is an article in which Mr. Freeman states that Black History Month should be deleted from the pillars of history.

Mr. Freeman went on record with this statement after Senator Barack Obama announced he was running for President of these United States. Now I don't know if Morgan Freeman had an inside track on facts showing Senator Obama was headed for a landslide victory and would become the First African-American President of this country. However, the distain of him uttering that statement still bewilders me to this day.

As African-Americans we are not completely out of that maze as of yet. Let us as a people stand tall and surely celebrate the victories we have accomplished since arriving on these shores in the sixteen hundreds. Let us celebrate the victories won since Honest Abe signed the *Emancipation Proclamation* in *Eighteen Sixty-Three*. By the way *Abolitionist Frederick Douglass* sat in the Oval Office with Mr. Lincoln giving advice on how to go about letting our people move to freedom.

Black History Week which came from the brilliant mind of *Mr. Carter G. Woodson* was brought to fruition to pay homage to blacks who were changing the course of history.

Eventually that week would become a month of celebrating our achievements. From that moment of time to this very moment in time, *Black History* is still being made and no way should we *(the generation upon this earth)* stand back and allow our children and their children suffer by not knowing their history.

It must be stated that our distinctive and rich history cannot and should not be deleted. We must mount up our knowledge base and once again disseminate this vital information to a generation that unfortunately believes that everything is given. Believe that they were the first and not only that, believe it is owed to them. The *Halls of Black History Fame* is filled with exciting periodicals of our great heroes who *fought, ran, marched, studied, invented, preached, teach, got whipped, hung, jailed, sung. Who was (is) entrepreneurs, raised, demonstrated, and prayed so we could be freed to enjoy a life of freedom* here on earth before going home to our maker.

In closing, I among many will trust our situation by agreeing *we have a rich history* and it's surely up to us to assure our Forefathers and Mothers are *kept alive,*

"BY ANY MEANS NECESSARY!"

Delete Black History? ***That's Insane!!*** We will not leave our future generations in the dark. Hooray for our *First Black President*, but don't get it twisted.

OUR HISTORY IS HERE TO STAY!!!

HAPPY BLACK HISTORY MONTH!!

THE END

13 STANDING OVATION

"I project that the world would be a better place if women were involved in every aspect of our world."
----------------Frederick Douglass, 1848.

The Question:
How far have our women come? How much have our women made an imprint into our world? This one goes out strictly to the *Ladies*.

Ladies if you are with me, **<u>Holler One Time!!</u>**

There is no denying without the birth of a woman we would not exist. When Adam laid down to rest, GOD Himself removed one of Adam's ribs to bring about a helpmate for him. That helpmate was in the form of a *wo-man*. Not to walk behind Adam, but yes, walk beside him. Be his mate who believed in and supported her man. Don't flip the script; it also helps when the man is supportive of his lady as well. It is also warmth when the man / gentleman is gentle enough to cater to his *Lady*.

As I grew older and did some homework, I discovered that the ancient Japanese had and still have a custom. When greeting a *Lady / woman* they would bow and remove their headgear in respect to her. Likewise, when about to enter a door or enter into a car, it's the *"Gentleman"* who would off er the kindness and address what was supposed to be done in favor of his *Lady*.

Saying that, not to put me on Front Street here, however after reading that, yes, I adopted that custom as well.

I think *(and nobody asked me what I think)* personally it is very manly and respectful for us men to be the better by acknowledging women in such a manner.

Sure, there will be some ladies who won't understand and there will be some who will laugh and think, *"The man is a trip gurl!"* Especially in this society today!!!

With the short space left, let's shift gears and further acknowledge our women here in the current. It seems everywhere I look women are stepping up to the plate, no longer are they being passive and taking the back seat. They have removed and moved to the front seat. No, it is not just our imagination, and this is not just for the single *Ladies*. *Ladies* with a ring on it as well have made a huge impact on this society. Women of all colors, cultures, and women from all over the world are standing tall and being heard as they shout out:

"I'M EVERY WOMAN, IT'S ALL IN ME!"

From the world of *motherhood, sisterhood, friendship, religion, education, business, entrepreneurship, entertainment, to putting eight hundred million cracks in the glass ceiling,* you women of the world are saluted for all you do every day. When there are clouds on the arising it's you and your trust in God who can pull through a situation. It's you *Ladies* who can garnish the love from those who seek in their worst hours. Take a grateful look at you this month. A ***"Standing Ovation"*** Is Due You!

"HAPPY WOMEN MONTH TO YOU"

THE END

14 W.I.N.N.E.R.

"A Winner never quit, and quitter never will Win!"

How many times during your lifetime have this popular saying squeezed and breezed by your ear drums? There is proof that you might have expressed these exact words to a youth, a family member, or just someone who might have been down on their luck at any given moment.

Well rest assure each *"24"* you are blessed to rise, know that your moment is about to blossom because of your hard work and your esteem of advancement to your next plateau. As in the award show state of mind, when it comes to announcing the winner the star about to make the presentation utter these words:

"envelope please…and the winner is……."

In this case the real winner is **"Y-O-U"** for your consistent drive and constantly getting the fullest out of each of your days.

Oh, it is definitely a challenge at times to get in that *Go Lane*, especially when issues tend to deliberately tackle your sense of purpose. Delivering an established amount of **"P.Y.B."** *(Pressing Your Buttons)* to your front door. Somewhere in your day's others have **P.Y.B.** causing an eruption rating from minimum to maximum and leaving them to bask in your **"H.B.P."** *(High Blood Pleasure)* escalating into the hemisphere.

A man who survived twenty-seven years in solitude to eventually becoming President of South Africa states:

Motivational Moments

"The secret to success is to learn to accept the impossible, to do without the indispensable and to bear the intolerable:"
---------------Nelson Mandela.

Exhibiting that fortitude of being able to transform self from the pessimistic issues to the optimistic renovator we were born to be.

Okay winner here is another ticket in the long line of successful information to help one stand tall on a daily and display a vision of a **CHAMPION!**

<u>**W**</u> – **WADE:** *Your destination could be compromises if you lose focus.*

<u>**I**</u> – **INDEPENDENT:** *Don't have a grievance against your uniqueness.*

<u>**N**</u> - **NOTICE:** *Use your 180-degree eye span in all your surroundings.*

<u>**N**</u> - **NATURAL:** *You are you! SUPERSTAR! Always be proud of yourself.*

<u>**E**</u> - **EXPRESSIVE:** *Spicy, Pizzazz, Eager, don't hide it, EXPRESS IT!*

<u>**R**</u> - **RISE:** *Give attention to the burning desires of your heart.*

By now you should get the legist:

*"<u>**W**</u>-<u>**I**</u>-<u>**N**</u>-<u>**N**</u>-<u>**E**</u>-<u>**R**</u>!!"*
How good is GOD?
He is *sooooooo good!*
He molded us into
"WINNERS!!"
"Got to Give it Up! Got to Live it Up!"
"WINNERS!!"

THE END

15 ARE YOU GREAT ENOUGH

In my latest reading, *"Become a Better You"* by Pastor Joel Osteen, my attention was captured when reaching page 21. That last paragraph! The last four lines was a defining moment thus far in Chapter 2, *"Give Your Dreams A New Beginning."*

What is the one dream that have been tagging you for the longest, and in return that dream steadily get ambushed, tackled and flung to the rear of your caboose? Ever tell yourself; *"I am living good enough."* In a Christian sense GOD did not and do not present good enough. In return we should not want to be so comfortable that we settle for good enough.

On a trip not long ago, to the Orlando Correctional Institute with Abe Brown Ministries, I was blessed to pray for and communicate with some pretty intelligent inmates who realized they made a terrible mistake. These individuals revealed that they are gifted with some awesome talents and gifts.

The shame of it all moving forth from their first day of incarceration to the day of their death, they will never get to see their dreams materialize in a real-world setting.

Turning the attention to those who are free to each day rise from the comfort of their luxury, the question is ask:
"Are you living good enough or are you seeking to be
"GREAT ENOUGH?"
Here is the disclaimer:
  In being *"Great Enough"* one must be able to forge forth despite what is popular.
  In being *"Great Enough"* one must be able to set their generation on fire by willing to set an extreme example for others to seek and follow.

In being **"Great Enough"** one must talk about being and display success of self and surroundings.

In being **"Great Enough"** one must (*at all cost*) encourage self in order to encourage those who seek encouragement.

In **"Great Enough"** one must as much as possible live the will of GOD and not the will of the mortal man.

Now the question again, ***ARE YOU WILLING TO BE:***

"GREAT ENOUGH?"

Keep this close to the frontal lope of your mind, there are millions of people who are enjoying their existence just being *"good enough!"* Each day is a *"whatever day,"* or each day is a *"same old thing, just another day!"* Knowing that we only get one pass in this life, one would think to want to run this race in the best mood and mode possible. Pulling out all the stops, get needed rest and needed rejuvenation, and once more press forth to your greatness.

The Mighty O'Jays told us to, *"Listen to the clock on the wall, it's getting closer to that hour!"* No, we don't know the hour, but each hour that tick *PUSH FORTH* with the power of being

"GREAT ENOUGH!"

Whatever you do, don't you be the poor soul who figured in your equation that "good enough" is how you will live your life. No, No, No, You Can't Take It No More, Living A Half Life. You Want Nothing But The Whole Thing. Because you are living:

"GREAT ENOUGH!!!!"

THE END

16 THE SUN, MOON & STARS

Have you ever heard of the old saying, *"be all you can be while you have the life to be?"* How about this one; *"the days are not promised so capture each moment!"* Just two microscopic shots of what the old folks would say back in the days. Of course, that was their way of inspiring us to reach for **the sun,** and **the moon,** and just in case we didn't make it to the sun or the moon, we could **land among the stars!!**

As youngsters we might have thought we could live forever and ever. Never believing we had a date with destiny. That may be one reason why those bible toting big mamas gave us those lessons, so we would get the very best out of our days and our life. We might not have known at the time that we would ultimately pass away. Better yet, Our Savior would be calling us home one day! Mama would say, *"We are only here for a short spell! Put your best foot forward in everything you do. If you fail maybe that is not the calling on your life. God got a special work for you; do it and happiness will find you. You might even go down in the history of man's books by following the commands of Jesus!"*

Many of men and women have gone on to their graves knowing that they left the best of them here on earth for another generation to follow in their great footsteps. Not just to follow in their great footsteps, but to curve off and create their own path and life for themselves, along with inspiring another generation to be motivated to hang out with **the sun, moon** and just in case they don't make it, **land among the stars!**

As a youngster what did you inspire to grow to be? Are you into your dream career of life today? If you are, are you truly preparing another generation to follow your path? Nothing and no one last forever!

Motivational Moments

Have you ever heard a successful person mum these words; *"I have done great in my lifetime and now I am ready to meet my Lord and Savior Jesus Christ?"* Maybe you have and maybe you have not. The moral is, this type of person has given him or herself to a cause greater than themselves. Doing the course of their time they lived a joyous life of output.

They spent a lifetime reaching for *the sun,* and *the moon.* To be honest all of them did not make it to *the sun,* or *the moon,* but you better believe they *landed among the "STARS!"*

Reflect back to the beginning of this story to the saying of old. Know it was those sayings that help the majority of a generation to be proud to rise each and every day and move forth to capture their quest.

"To Dream The Impossible Dream"
To fight when arms are too weary. To march through hell with a heavenly pulse. To know if only being true to a glorious quest, that the world scold and cover with scares still strove with its last ounce of courage. To follow that star, no matter how hopeless, no matter how far. To reach the unreachable
"STARRRRRRRRRRRR!"
---------- Writer Joe Darion

While you have life are you using it to attempt to reach **THE SUN** or perhaps **THE MOON?** If you don't for some reason, it's ok if you land among;

"THE STARS!!!"

THE END

17   **F. I. F. A.**

"As we strive to make it through tough times, hearing the wisdom of those who struggled, questioned and dreamed before us can make the journey easier."
……..Beliefnet.com

Well you know where we are right about now. The employment situation, got to wait until August before the oil situation is capped, more housing is sitting vacant and Petro is fluctuating constantly. Don't even discuss what is aired these days in primetime *(8 to 11pm)*. Forget it; don't even touch the eleven o'clock evening news.

A crisis and a lesser belief, *definitely a negative tongue!* It resembles listening to a talking head and believing their every word. While discussing political issues it was said the majority of the GOP has voters warped; hanging on false statements without properly seeking truth through research, and resources. So, rebelling with negation is the response.

History tells us this is not America's first journey down this dark and narrow road. It also tells us strength is essential in this type of climate. The wisdom of those who been through passed it on to the generation of now, *just do it* and *believe in your God* and likewise *believe in yourself* and eventually you too will *crest in victory*.

What is F.I.F.A.? If you are familiar with World Cup Soccer yearly event that take place, *(RAH, RAH,* **GO USA!***)* you will know that *FIFA* stands for:

"Federation International Football Association"

In this content **F.I.F.A.** is the acronym for:

(**F**) - *FACETIOUS* – don't become victims of the crisis; know God will bring the breakthrough. Keep a joyful heart and a form of amusement while going through this downturn.

(**I**) – *INCREMENT* – build up fortitude of your *mind, body, soul* and *spirit* to know all good things happen for the sake of the Lord. ***"U R A GOOD THING & GOOD THINGS ARE HAPPENING FOR YOU NOW!!!"***

(**F**) – *FERVANT* – Continue to be passionate about your goal of making you & your family a daily success. You got to be tough in this crisis. God will calm the waters, *let go and let God!*

(**A**) – *APPEARANCE* – They say appearance is everything, however, demonstrate the need for help that will extend your vision of fortune coming to fruition. Know what is relevant and irrelevant!

A crisis is the test to make you or break you. Honestly, you can't aff ord to break, somebody is depending on **Y.O.U.**!

Let's play, bring on the ***F.I.FA.!***

THE END

18 WHAT'S IN YOUR CLOSET

While you are out on any gifted day from God, remember that you are going to encounter people. People, who will represent a variety of moods ranging from being terribly upset at the world, just upset in general, and mad at the world! This could include being in a timid mood, shy mood, and a not being bothered mood. How about those you will cross who are in a happy, jovial, celebrating mood (*posing a disguise*). These are some of the character moods we cross on daily.

The question is: What do we possess in our closet that can and will boost the morale of another. You may be familiar with the over the counter product, *5-hour energy,* once consumed; the *two - thirty eff ect* is defeated. True to fold in the midst of our fast pace days we all can use a hand from another's internal closet. Let the true story be told, many can't and don't know how to wheel and deal within their own mental domain.

There are numerous reasons for the shortcomings of many. We are the executives of our closets, know what is lying dormant or just hovering within that can serve as a life saving device for one falling prey to the pressure. Oh, how gifted are thee having a perimeter that ward off distressful crisis; therefore, aff ording the fortunes of staying sane. On the back of this issue, some who lack a perimeter to ward off such crisis find temporary relief by faking it, some sweat it out by displaying a tempestuous air of disturbance, some fuse it out by the foulness of their mouth, some quench it out by living in the bottle, and some high it out by tripping daily on cloud nine.

"All Are Defeating Remedies!"

Motivational Moments

"Ready or not we can't hide, it's in our closet" especially when there is a cry for the dishing out and making a diff erence in a recoiled life. Let it be written plain and simple, people like us have something to off er to the less fortunate. *Less fortunate?* People who have the internal riches however, their tension is registering so high on the rector scale that contents of bountiful gifts turn into a shameful waste. The unfortunate is subject to believing riches are all about external gains.

The majority of our raging desires are stored internally and with the right scope of how to infuse those riches will ultimately lead to many situations where we become the benefactor!

Peering into a tiny opening, it is seen big as the pupils can see. There it is, it is called;

"L-O-V-E!"

Somewhere in the closet of your internal self is that mechanism triggering a motion, and an action. It set you in motility mode to kindle humility by extending a line of hope graciously. Our closet is an association of aspiring assurance not just to self, but yes, to others seeking a hand. If used in a fraction of righteous our perks are breathtaking.

"Don't keep your closet locked!!

Maybe what's in your closet is a lifesaver for one who is drowning. Everyday make it a priority to lend a helping hand. Speak highly of another. Be a joy to someone who need what you are hiding within. *Share, SHARE* alike!!

"WHAT IS IN YOUR CLOSET??"

THE END

19   RING, RING GO THE BELL

"Up in the morning and out to school the teacher is teaching the golden rule."
----- Chuck Berry, Rock and Roll Singer

It is time our children return to the classrooms to foster growth of knowledge, character and conduct. Time again for the staff of dedicated teachers to prepare lessons that will hopefully direct our young students to academic achievement.

Pronouncing and highlighting reading, writing, and solving math problems will serve as the manuscript to a healthy learning style, which in turn leads to a greater number of our youth with cap and grown validation.

For our youth to achieve this rim of success, *parents you will have to be on alert!* Yes, it is understood *parents have work obligations, parents may be minus transportation,* and there are numerous other reasons why a parent can't be there for their children.

Whatever the case just stop and think what is occurring as you are minus in your child all important school years. This is not saying without parents our children are failures, *this is not the notion,* however with you, *your child has a better chance of reaching the next level of conquering their endeavor of graduating with true education in tow!*

Parents it is going to take as much of your participation in assisting your loving child to be a successful student in this / their succeeding in their studies.

Through the decades it has been our youth toting the pail systematically and consistently at the lower periphery of the educational scale.

As a person concerned about the educational nurturing of your child it will be pertinent that a major role is played by you, *parent*. If a child must ride old big yellow across town, it can't *be "it's too far;"* it can be *"I'm determined to find a way to check on my child."*

When a child says, "no homework," it is the *parent's* responsibility of *"creating homework,"* not neglect and let television, smartphones, Xbox, videos or the freedom of hanging out be the dominator. With our children in this arena of today with so many distractions, it's a must that we step up to our biggest challenge and be *"our children biggest advisory!"*

Reading articles on the dropout rates and non-graduation rates concerning our *African-American Males* and *Hispanic Males* show deplorable numbers that we as a community have to stay on point and adhere to in order for our youth to have a grace of an opportunity to be counted in the numbers of graduation instead of *numbers across their uniform!*

Prisons, Built for Black & Hispanic Youth!
This shouldn't be chatter swept under a bridge!

Let's make the commitment for our children & our students to further thier steps and assure the success of our children in the classroom. Take proactive steps & our young will be *intelligent, and successful* Graduates!

"OUR CHILDREN ARE PRIORITY!"

THE END

20   FINDING FAVOR

"So shalt thou find favor and good understanding in the sight of God and man."
Proverbs 3:3 vs 4.

What is a **FAVOR?**
Have you ever done a **FAVOR** for someone?
How true is it that you are living in **FAVOR?**
Do **FAVOR** really exist?
What's up with the questions and what's really up with
"F-A-V-O-R?"

Specifically, once a person decides to eclipse a rude life of destructive behavior and divert towards a life of sensibility, a spectacular occurrence begin to take place.

Living with unselfish means and being a deliverer as opposed to a person outfitted in chaos with a taker's character, adds up to a sufficient amount of grace and a garden of healthy blessings.

FAVOR - Automatic like an escalator providing an ease when your tired body can't climb the stairs.

FAVOR - How about when you are treated to a red carpet affair! Think on these things and emerge realizing the discovery of advantage of express!

"WOW, TRUE THAT!"

On a Sunday not too far gone an associate and I shared some words about our lives of days gone by; *"Club Dayz."*

He mentioned he was not aware of the reasoning for his still standing strong these days. He then went on to recognize Prayer and *"FAVOR!"* My response was simple, *FAVOR* can be a life journey, and we must be obedient and handle the responsibility of being in and of *FAVOR!*

Didn't know *FAVOR* came with *Responsibility*? Ask some of the folks, who tried to take advantage of *FAVOR*! Hear and see their fall from grace. Think about the many that unfortunately are no longer with us because they decided to misuse *FAVOR*!

Even in my spin of life, I too were abound and at times my thirteen pound head begin to enlarge because I mistakenly had a vision that it was all about me. (*can anybody relate*)!

Proverbs 3:3 vs 4 is a great verse to familiarize self with; having the comforts of *FAVOR* brings about a certain goodwill and generosity far beyond what one can comprehend. Now comprehend being in a zone and, and on the receiving end of *"thou are highly favored!"* That is a blessing within itself, agree?

Embrace the privileges that are approved, sanctioned and in line with:
    F - *F*aith reinforced.
    A – *A*ttitude for solidarity.
    V – *V*oice of merit.
    O – *O*bserving with wisdom.
    R - *R*eaction in humility.

Make a point to   **N.F.L.**
*(Navigate **FAVOR** in your Lifetime).*
Guarantee to be a splendid situation of satisfaction!

THE END

21 THANKS-GIVING

How many ways can we illustrate a *Give?*
How many ways can we illuminate a *Thanks?*

There are several variations of these two significant action words. They speak to the *respect* and *appreciation* for what has or what is about to be done for someone.

It is noted in the ages of time we are a very *Giving* and *Thankful* people whose dedication has afforded us many blessings. Just typing this story brings to mind a peek into visions of our lineage on the great shores from the motherland where *Thanks* and *Giving* no doubt was present. To clarify so the above statement is not taken out of content, within those ships, sure harsh treatments was prevalent; however, glance at what our ancestors bridged through to get their lineage positioned for a recent historical event chartered into our current state of life.

Viewing the big picture, would one rather be on the vessels engrossed in trials of great magnitude or entangled in a flourishing life headlined with unknown possibilities?

As an African-American culture living in this age of constant tension, let us take a break from the briskness of the hustle and bustling that seem to keep us afloat. Hey, getting our grind on is the joint, you know that grind allow for us to enjoy the luxury of certain enjoyable wants and for sure it allows us our needs, *and you know we got needs!*

Here we are faced with two important occasions. The first one, most definitely we "need" to adhere to is "VOTE!" If you are aware of our history, man, talk about being Thankful?

The way our ancestors were treated just because they wanted to cast a vote, *"GIVE ME A BREAK!!"*

Don't mention not casting your vote. *"Why should I vote, it don't benefit me (**Heartache with a capital H**)."* Eyes reading this and having a negative thought about voting, heed this: ***"Don't Vote, Don't Complain, and You Don't Count!" Furthermore, it's Injustice to your Children and Theirs!!!***

"THANKSGIVING," which is the second important occasion, arrives in November, the last Thursday to be exact. It's the time we convene with Family and just *Give Thanks* for all that has transpired in our life. It's the time we recognize how important it is to have people who love us for who we really are. It's time we give *Thanks* for the goodness GOD has bestowed upon us. Some of us lost love ones, however in their lost; we *Give Thanks* to the fact of them inspiring our daily being. It's a time we acknowledge our children no matter their success or their failures. I'm not even going to mention the many dishes that will be prepared. *"The Dishes Is Smart Stuff "* compared to the many Blessings that can be conjured up and shared by each family member. So be Blessed and Enjoy!

Lastly, I bid everyone a

"HAPPY THANKS – GIVING!"

THE END

22   10

    Five as in five years plus five years take us to the total sum of ten (10) years which is the ending of another Decade. Any time within these ten years did you find yourself reciting the famous phrases, *"wow where did the time go,"* or *"I just can't believe we got here so quick."* Maybe it was, *"time doesn't wait on anyone."* Whatever the case you will agree, we are here and thank God for allowing us to see this time in our life.

    Allow me some reflection time as we prepare to once again be blessed to see another year going forward. Can you remember the rage that was set in motion and had an America racing? The belief Y2K was the signal the world is headed to destruction as we knew it. One thing for sure Prince's song *"Party Like It's 1999"* create a party zone as we flipped our calendars to what would become a very historical decade in our life. Who phantom the path we as a country and we as a people would eventually find ourselves on at that junction? Between the year of our Lord 2000 and the year of our Lord 2010 some pretty remarkable occurrences took place that more or less influences how we live our life today. Imagine what has taken place and what has happened in all of our lives over the last nineteen years. It darned on me a week ago that we are putting another decade to sleep. To be honest the original title for this story was "12" however during reflection I couldn't help but to think past the months of 2010 and envision the panorama picture of two decades that swiftly disappeared and *2020 larking!*

    For the sake of "10" I will attempt to revisit some major events taking place during this period of time. You may remember some of the events mentioned and then again maybe not.

Motivational Moments

You may also want to think of major events that took place in your life over the span of time.

2000 (*a leap year*) came in on a Saturday and we survived the Y2K scare. As we tried to settle into the new 21st Century, fireworks started igniting with The Bush Brothers (*Governor Jeff and President George*) creating a stir and such a fiasco that it threw us in a whirlwind (*the elections*). Moving forth we got a rude awaken *with Katrina, 9-11, The Haiti Earthquake, Enron, The Economic Downturn, The Columbian Spaceship, Iraq, Afghanistan, and America electing the First Black President.* Oh, how our conversation continued to change as the *Pop Culture* front saw the demise of the CD and the growth *of Digital iTunes*. From a large box to an *LCD T.V.* hanging on your wall, *Reality Shows* corralled our interest and *Rap* has taken a spin into our every fiber that streams from commercial advertising to *The Pope*. Of course, in the Life God has called home some very notable celebrities, too numerous to do a roll call. Surely in our personal families we have all lost a few love ones as well.

As we say goodbye to a historical occurrence of time, let us pray for the next decade emerging quickly, beginning with *"2020."* Betting on God to grant us the staying power to continue to better ourselves and the world.

AMEN

HAPPY NEXT "10" YEARS, 2020!!!!!

THE END

23   **IN WITH THE NEW**

"Get Up, Get Down, Get Up On Your Feet"
---------The Dramatics

The stroke of midnight brings to this world a new hour, new day and of course a new year. As Americans we know the drill, the night of New Year's Eve become a split decision. Meaning some will party the night away, some will give praise to GOD for another year of life, some will relax at home with family, and of course some of us will decide to wreak havoc. However, you might have decided to spontaneously spend your New Years, realize *we are in with the new!*

Each year it is noted that we, creatures of habit will plan to begin a holistic healthy regime. We plan to expand our horizon with furthering our education, maybe advancing within our employment field, how about volunteering, or becoming an entrepreneur.

The national survey says a minor instead of the majority of us will carry out our New Year's Resolution.

Whatever goals you might have set or are foreseeing to come to fruition in this year, let me share some worthwhile information that just might help in your new living.

Since we are **"IN WITH THE NEW"**

"In all thy ways acknowledge him, and he shall direct thy paths. Proverbs 3:6. This will fortify you for those moments of adversity that will surely find its way to your domain.

If you have not already, start to live a *"PURPOSE DRIVEN LIFE!"* Know why you are blessed to be living. Find your calling and become proactive by helping others to live in a similar fashion.

"AFFIRMACISE," as you brace for a new experience at the local gym, also affirmacise your mind with daily doses of powerful and practical supplements which will decree truth in your life.

Use your *"ACTION SIGNALS"* to stay in a vibrate mode. Intelligently deal with situations attempting to alter your feelings and emotions. Stop negative emotions in its tracks!

"Shake the tree of life and bring down fruit unheard-of!"
-------- E.A. Robinson
Stand strong and command your presence, it's yours, *why not!*

"TAKE RISKS & BE ADVENTURESOME!" Really use this to the fullest by not becoming complacent with a new variation of monotone and comfort - ability.
Success is inversatility.

Be a *"HIGHLY EFFECTIVE PERSON"* which will lay the ultimate respect upon your shoulders, you will be of greater value to those who value your intellect and know how.

Have *"FAITH, COURAGE, INSIGHT & VIEW!"* Life will lead you strictly by your perceptions. Continue your days by staying on point and surely you will enjoy the fruits.

"Stumbling and groping through the wilderness finally must be replaced by a planned, organized, and orderly march."

THE END

24   OUR ACHIEVEMENTS

    1926 in celebration of Frederick Douglass and Abraham Lincoln's birthday, **CARTER G. WOODSON (1875-1950)** launched **"NEGRO HISTORY WEEK"** which didn't turn into **"BLACK HISTORY MONTH"** until *February 1976*, when it was extended into the whole *"28" days"* of ***February!***

    Wake Up, Wake Up it's the most important month of the year for our black experience. This is the month that we cannot have the Miseducation of our Negro People *(C.G.W. 1933)!*

    Though our history expands the whole *365 days* of the year, it is the 28 days of this month that all the research, teaching, exploring and discoveries of our people are displayed so those generations behind us will not be left out in the cold.

    In recent years it's noticed the populace through politically correct meager are attempting to dilute BHM and add a flare that decreases the true knowledge being distributed and taught like Mr. Woodson meant it to be. *Don't be hood winged!* As the phase goes, ***"don't know where we come from, how we gonna know where we as a people are going?"***

    Let not our ignorance about our own contributions be a scene such as the statue of Booker T. Washington removing the covers off a slave *(on the campus of Tuskegee University)* who sees freedom for the first time. Through the channels of American history African-Americans have hailed many celebrations of accomplishments. We in today's society can and should draw upon our forefathers & foremothers. For instance, in short, **Alice Walker** the eighth child of a sharecropper entertaining us with the *Color Purple*. **Henry Louis Gates** credited for helping us through *DNA*, find *Our True Ancestry*.

Motivational Moments

Eunice Johnson credited for our enjoying the *Ebony Fashion Fair*. The **C. Blythe Andrews** family beginning in 1919 to the present, educating *West Central Floridians* with their *Florida Sentinel Bulletin*. **Rev. Leon Lowry** served as the *First African-American* on *Hillsborough County Public School Board*, besides teaching a young man named **Martin Luther King, Jr.** at *Morehouse College* in the 1940's.

In Wimauma, Florida there is an elementary school as of 2008 that bear the name of **Doris Ross Reddick** who served as the *First Black Woman* on the *Hillsborough County School Board* and the first black to teach at *Thonotosassa Elementary School*. **Otis Anthony** the *First* to *Write the History of Tampa's African-Americans* as well being the *First Black* in *Tampa Bay* to serve as *Assistant Mayor of Tampa*, plus be selected for a *National Urban Fellow* and lastly, **Darryl & Tammy Johnson** also brought us a first, *The N-Touch Newspaper & The Power Couple Ball*. Like clockwork they keep us abreast to what we as people are into as well what's happening in Tampa Bay. Finally there is **Sherryl Cusseaux** who each year, proudly delivers *The DSI Black Pages*.

This is just a tidbit of reasons why we can and should continue our campaign of feeling inordinately optimistic about our feats which surely continues to this very day. We are in agreement with living the light of hope, however we surely must fight the good fight as time transform us to the future while developing a safe haven for;

"OUR ACHIEVEMENTS"

THE END

25   **A MAN**

"A man born innocent in a turbulent, demeaning, painful, abusive situation find himself harmful, hateful, killing, suicidal & boastful to mankind and a companion to the most low, Satan!"

    A man awakens to find *GOD* and *Blessings* upon him. Find no fault but, find the will power to reinvent self in the name of *JESUS CHRIST!* Humble himself in the presence of GOD & Mankind to be used as a vessel to empower many!

    A man takes on life with a new *vigor, moral principles, happiness & serious focus of a conqueror*! He carries out the will of GOD and the will of self to assist in elevation of a lost, broken, confused & abused person!

    A man, do that make him better than the next human being, the next man, woman, boy or girl? *"NO!"* It makes him fulfilled with *Faith, Purpose, Integrity, Beamed Willingness, Agility* to put forth his best regardless of the circumstances.

    A man finds the *Truth & Spirit* from on high to live his life on altitude despite what may come. *No excuses,* no need to fabricate, *responsible for own actions.* A man of personal account, a man standing strong on conviction, *no matter what society try or attempt to convince him to believe or accept!*

    A man who smile, a friend of the world, no enemies, non-afraid, standing for justice, *the man is aware of his standards.* He doesn't pound on another's beliefs or lifestyle, just know if it isn't of GOD, *it is not of him!*

    A man at the mercy of JESUS CHRIST for bringing him through. He, knowing love desires love.

Desire love with principles within the boundaries of *health, prosperity* & *living at the pinnacle.*

A man prays this day for each and every man and every woman of this life who are an over comer of the most worst abuse at the hands of another & themselves. *Don't never give up and bow to anyone except the most high!*

Live each of your days with elevated sense of purpose. Worry not about what others say about you! Know you are of greatness to live at your most intense moments.

Life is short, live long in your days. Turn the media box off, turn on an awesome empowering movie, or CD. Plug in the most inspiring sermon to build self-confidence. Help the less fortunate, the unable, the disabled. Be a friend to the friendless. *Awaken to breathe and inhale /exhale of your existence. Run, stretch & exercise! Run pain, soreness, disease, misery, nonsense, excuse away and live as healthy as possible!*

A man exit negative people, family & ones who which to hold him down. *Those who have a negative view of you, a jealous view of you, a pessimistic view of you, and who use you for their gain.* Those who are backstabbers, move them from your view! Keep in mind as you walk this life, a man is no island! However, surround self with those who are jubilant and optimistic of your success. Not haters of your success! *Embark on a role model, mentor, who honestly want your growth!*

Lastly, A man who is blessed don't mind sharing his blessings with others only if they are appreciative of the share. A man of good nature is destined of a good and blessed life for self and others!

"A MAN"
THE END

26 GREAT

What's *soo* good about ***GREAT?***

GREAT *GOD*!
GREAT *JESUS CHRIST*!
GREAT *BLESSINGS*!
GREAT *FAITH*!
GREAT *LOVE*!
GREAT *LIFE*!
GREAT *MIND*!
GREAT *KNOWLEDGE*!
GREAT *FEELINGS*!
GREAT *HEALTH*!
GREAT *SPIRIT*!
GREAT *ASPIRATIONS*!
GREAT *STORMS*!
GREAT *PAIN*!
GREAT *GAIN*!
GREAT *THOUGHTS*!
GREAT *FRIENDS*!
GREAT *ASSOCIATIONS*!
GREAT *FAMILY*!
GREAT *MOTIVATION*!
GREAT *MENTORS*!
GREAT *REST*!
GREAT *BELIEFS*!
GREAT *THANKFUL*!
GREAT *PHYSICAL*!
GREAT *INTERNAL*!
GREAT *BUSINESS*!
GREAT *FOCUS*!
GREAT *RESPECT*!
GREAT *RESULTS*!
GREAT *AGE*!

GREAT *CAREER*!
GREAT *PURPOSE*!
GREAT *PASSION*!
GREAT *MISSION*!
GREAT *FULFILLMENT*!
GREAT *I FEEL GREAT*!
GREAT *BEGINNING*!
GREAT *CONCLUSION*!
GREAT *MORNING, NOON, NIGHT*!
GREAT *ENDINGS*!

THE REASONS TO LIVE IN *GREATNESS!*
THE SIMPLE REASONS TO LIVE IN HAPPINESS!
THIS IS REASON FOR FORGIVENESS!
FIND *GREATNESS* AND GREAT OCCURANCE WILL APPEAR!
SHATTER THE PATH TO DOOMVILLE WITH THE FEELING OF *GREATNESS!*
MANY HAVE ACHIEVED THROUGH *GREATNESS!*
SURE, HARD WORK PAYS OFF IN THE PURSUIT OF *GREATNESS!*
WAKING UP IN THE MORNING IS THE FILLING OF *GREATNESS!*
BUILD THE LADDER TO YOUR SUCCESSFUL *GREATNESS!*
TACKLE YOUR 55,000 THOUGHTS WITH YOUR *GREATNESS!*

BORN INTO THIS WORLD WHY NOT LIVE IT WITH *GREATNESS!*
SHARE WITH ANOTHER WHO LACK OR MAY LACK *GREATNESS!*
CARESS IT! IT'S A WONDERFUL ENDEAVOR OF *GREATNESS!*
AN EAGLE OF *GREATNESS!*

THE END

27   WILL OVERCOME

Whatever Temperament may be your blockage!
Whatever past situations gripping you!
Whomever may be standing firm in your path!
Today is not "DREAM DEFERRED DAY!"
Today is: *"DREAM PROACTIVE DAY!"*

    See, feel, adapt to maximizing your potential! Turn your baby steps into giant steps of presentation! Don't give your negative an up on your positive! Park your naysayers who challenge your drive! The championship of your desires is hungry! Are you feeding the pessimistic you?

Are you starving the optimistic you?

    Stay off the hamper of despair. Stay on the hamper of glory in accomplishment! Day one is your distinguish birth. All million and some days you must conquer. All those nights rest in the arms of our Savior. That your mornings are joyful and earnest to boot! Put in the grind to confess your grenade of a star. Look down your road, see your end. Now what do you discover before it's said? Empty due to expelling your every fiber? Maybe full from living a wasted existence? The choices of elevation or flat line?

    This is it; total is the sum of your best. *Cry, Try, By, Shy, Sigh!* Whatever the case. Don't leave on full. Visual the generations to come and onslaught from afar. Don't let them starve for lack of your bondage knowledge. You are the manifest giving to disseminate the applied information that add to civilization. This is crude of the tide washed to shine in diamond!

Motivational Moments

Don't discount your motivational prowess on self and another. You are born with wealth of calculated millions to thrust higher. It might be the lesser strength on their lesser days of hoping elevation. You, You, Mr. or Ms. *Ultimately Shine On Them!* Lift their spirits as your spirit was lifted to embrace the fine tell of self-acceptance.

Adorable it is, "YOU" are enhancing and transforming a person's gloom into gleam so they too can feel the eff ects of serious inspiration within their day after day.

Acknowledge the percentage in the column accounting accomplishments upon self-belief! All you have to have is the gall to dedicate self in a fashion that pays dividends to having endurance. *The Payoff ?* ***"UNIQUE!"***

As written in the Good Book,
"If you can believe, as things are possible to those who believe." Hey this is the road that ride you on the thoroughfare, breezing you forward to the benefit of the *"YOU SHALL OVERCOME!"* Extraordinary in a cheerful state of mind, and person due to the payment made over - coming those past challenges to revel in the shine!

At this stage intensify a laugh of liberty and leadership that scopes the internal being. Open your door carefully to the external spectrum as to illuminate the dark which a majority hover daily.

WE / YOU / ME / THEM / CAN / ***"WILL OVERCOME"***

JUST DEEPLY BELIEVE, BELIEVE!!!!

THE END

28   DON'T WANT NOBODY

    Many have fought the good fight before traveling to glory. They sweat and strained! Filled the buckets with pain! Bargained for the sense of light & carried many loads up the road of history. We would be hundredpercent wrong not being enhanced with motivation.

    Don't lie, a few are hiding with disgrace! Ashamed because they are prisoners of procrastination! Maybe even worse, prisoners of a negative mind or having memory loss of how successful they really are, and can be.

    That's right the battle has been fought for you and me! No need to gripe over the small crumbs. Keep in mind it's the large willingness awaiting your entrance. Kick off those complacent shoes and replace them with shoes of affirmed action. Take off those garments of denial. Transfer into garments that spur you to the hemisphere of fulfilling your goals.

    This is it! Stand, Stand to the eastern shower of a new U! Hack with waiting, waiting become past tense fast!

"NOW IS NOW & NOW MUST BE NOW"
NO TOMORROW - "NOW!"

    Listen to the tick - tock. Oh yea it's ticking faster and faster! Do nothing is not and never is the answer to progress. Those of Old - School could not afford to sit on their yesterday, and neither can you, we or I! Get up if sitting down and stretch it out. *Fire up your molecules of zest for life.* Yearn for the grateful abilities that jolly in the presence of *"Y-O-U!"*

    Listen there are enough people on this earth, this United States getting up from bed every single day with no purpose.

Motivational Moments

They speak, *"What you gonna do"* or *"what they are not going to do because they don't want to and don't have to!"* Hate to spoil the party, but in order to achieve, one must push forward with positive belief in self! You don't believe in self –

"NO ONE WILL!!!"

Accurately concentrate on being active in life to exceed your own expectations by humbly zooming in on the prize that is in reality, yours. There is one fault that can and will delete you from holding *the prize*. What may be holding me from the prize of flourishing? *Complaining, Blaming, Passing the baton* are just a few ways to stop your progress and cut you short. Have bravado, erect and stand firmly with the magic of intention on succeeding at all cost! Begin living in the art of appreciation of your reason for being. Take those moments of still and allow the ease of thought on what you can and will accomplish with experience and excitement of your abilities to actually live the life you expect!

Hey, this can be *Heaven* and for real, it can be *your worst Hell!* You have to Choose which you would like to live in, *ASAP! "CHOICES!"* We all have them! Live without the chains that surely steal progression. The title says it all, ***"Don't Want Nobody!"*** It's not up to anybody but you!

"Don't Want Nobody To Give Me Nothing, I'll Get It Myself"
(a James Brown hit)!"

STOP the Procrastination and go for yours!

THE END

29   GET IT, GET IT

Rising to the occasion of your greatness. An everyday thing it should be. Left with one option, *the best of you!* Like an optic vision.

Straight like an arrow hitting its target, feeling amplified as to seek satisfaction. The key, not settling in a cave of displeasure like some do. Acknowledging your shortcomings and rectifying your calculated moves. *Power Up* on assertion of gravity.

Seems of late all the Champions are dead!
Wait, *Who are U?*
Wait, *Who am I?*
    "CHAMPIONS, CHAMPIONS!!!"

Living & Moving, *Energetic Champions!*
Giving in, **"NEVER!"** Quitting, **"NEVER!"**
Crying tears of pain into gain.
Can you feel it?
Rising to the Feelings!
Pumping the Heart!
Pumping the Mind!
Pumping you to exceed the norm!
Easy Now Easy!!!!!!!!
Did I say Easy?

"GRIND BABY GRIND, GRIND ON!" YEEESSSSSSSS!

Recently it was told to me, *DLD* you are done, your days have passed! Lay back and relax now, you earned it! My response: Long as GOD give me breath and health there is no lay back and relax. *Never submit to complacent and comfortable ideas.*

Motivational Moments

To those type of thinking, I also say, *Thank you very much my Friend!* Thank you for the *"Rejuvenation!"*

Stay in the game of life as long as you can. That's right, *as long as you can!!!* Stand the test of time by reinventing yourself with your God Given Talents. Be inspired to install a new you into view. *Be bold, place you on the front page of your headline newsletter.* Don't get it twisted, it's not about the bragging, for the most part it's about your hang time. Hang time you may wonder?

Sure, let me explain, in tempting to reinvent self it may seem as if there are many mountains, doors to defeat. In reality it all relies on your persistence to overcoming your past, to travel to your prosperous future. Which can be time consuming and well worth the eff ort. Do you have the tenacity?

We all fail at something, we all come short at something. On the other hand, *we defeat, we win, we conquer, we victorious, we triumph, we activate, we action, we achieve.* Guess you get the idea. With determination and staying keen to focus, the quest will be secured. The question is, are you willing to put in the work?

There are more successful financially set people than there are those who quit! Those that use every moment to find a problem instead of a solution. There they are, are you destined to be one of the problems or are you destined to be supreme with solutions? If so *"GET IT, GET IT NOW!"*

Not tomorrow, next week, next month or next year!
"SHINE U UP!"   &   *"GET IT, GET IT!"*
"DON'T QUIT!"

THE END

30   **DONE**

Go ahead, lay down and call your life quit! Struggling through your days and nights. Dealing with exceptional pain every second. To add, everything, everything you touch crinkle into tiny pieces. So, go ahead throw in the white towel!!!!

A glimpse of the agony we go through as we live. Only a select few realize the challenge and like a bolt of lightning shoot far past the lay down and they are off never to falter by the mishaps of life.

What makes a physically challenged *(in whatever case you may think of)* continue to thrive despite their circumstance. "WHAT?" It's the Will Power, yes, the *WILL POWER!!* These people don't know the word done; they know despite their circumstances they will continue to try at every turn! I'm talking about with every fiber in their *heart, mind, soul and body*. If they have to go, it is not because they did not give their all each and every day!!!

Some may not like the following statement however here it is. Those people that are wheelchair bound or dealing with some type of major disease are truly my inspiration. Losing an uncle from the illness of diabetes motivated me to want to take better care of myself. A person with high blood pressure, cancer and heart disease *(high cholesterol which is my issue)* are my signals to pay even closer to what I consume, what I drink and eat. It propels me to hit the gym and work as hard as I do. *Leaving it all on the field!* It's a great feeling to hear my doctors tell me how impress they are with my great health for my age.

Are you considering being "DONE?"
Don't fall prey to a pessimistic mind of self-worth.

If not careful, and in control of your mind, you say hello to sickness, grievance, negative outlook and despair, this will most likely be followed by the demise of you literally, figuratively & physically! This is better known as D-O-N-E, *"DONE!!!!"*

If it's you reading this with low self esteem, as I had to learn and speak into existence, *The battle is not mine,* I had to *release and let GOD fight my battles.*

Despite wanting to be done, I had to turn to where my help come from. No other than *"MY LORD AND SAVIOR!"* That was first and foremost! From there I had to transform self to be in the company of people who have a sensation for life and who also have that **WINNING ALTITUDE** about the life they live! No, No way could I have thrown in the towel! I admit, sure at times I wanted to throw in the towel. As I look back over the last twenty years, if the towel would have been thrown in, at this age I may not be in my right mind. Instead of writing this book, who is to say, I might be on my last leg of life. Who knows, could be in the casket heading six feet under!

Make up your mind how you want to live. At a certain point one must get past the blame of their environment. The blame of their shortcomings. The blame of someone else! The blame of self is the issue that need to be resolved in order to live the ideal life you desire. Know where you are and where you wish to go.

Giving up instead of pushing forth is a sin that will leave you disgruntled. So, accept the challenge and stand up to create infinite tranquility of a thriving self-being.

DON'T NEVER BE "DONE!"
THE END

Motivational Moments

31   BEST LOVE

It can accrue on a Sunny Day. How about on a Cloudy Day? Maybe at the Crack of Dawn? Definitely when having a talk with GOD! It is better than the dollar you grip.
Twice as better overwhelming the luxury you drive!
Darn, Get This, *Spurring Faster than Love of Nutrition!*

"BEST LOVE"

Some travel life without a trace of it. Not even recognizing it staring bright! Taking Frustration into a Boiler Room.
Blowing Fuses into Explosions.
Blind to the cause of the dismantling.
The Question is how can one exist minus it?
You better beware, those type will
Destruct in a mini-second!
Who become the victims, *U & I!*

"BEST LOVE"

NORA ROBERTS mentioned what you want, you'll never have it. If you don't ask, the answer is always no. If you don't step forward, you will always be in the same place!

SHINING BY FAR REPRESENT GLEAM!
Not gloom & doom!
NOT THROWING IN THAT SURRENDER!
Get out *Won! It Actually Won!!!!*
Send that gloom, frustration, disgust, directly packing south!
As the March Wind blow use it to
CLEANSE OF NEGATIVITY!
The adventure will be a total advantage.

"BEST LOVE"

It is a cheering occasion, You must be *"U!"*
Can you feel the excitement taking its place upon the sight of *U?*
Captivate in the solace with purity. It's you with
LOVE X U LOVE!

"BEST LOVE"

This Now, This Second, This Rising!
Not allowing it to pass you in thought.
If not already now is the exact minute to ***SELF LOVE U!***
Initiate it and your inbox will overflow!
Overflow like a tidal wave of joy!
Those not at your spiral case definitely will wonder &
wonder until their beam tickle!

"BEST LOVE"

Go the height of it!
Wrap you in it!
Mount Everest is a scope away, ***REACH IT!***
Move forth once secured in it! *Share! Share!* A like, *not as a novice.*

"BEST LOVE"

Today is truly suffering due to lack of
SELF – LOVE, INFINITE-LOVE, ESTEEM –LOVE,
& HONEST–LOVE!
These LOVES ARE ON LIFE SUPPORT!
We must be *THE SURGEONS* AND *RESURGE THE LOVE!*
WE ARE IN NEED OF
"BEST LOVE"

THE END

CONCLUSION

RETROSPECT

The beginning and end of this writing has finally come. The "Begin" was far from the final word to forward to you, the awaiting reading fans. When the beginning process started it was figured there would be no problem completing this book in a timely manner. Oh, not the case!

As we all know, *"life happens!"* When life happens, we tend to get off course of our mission at hand due to we must tend to the matters that are very important. It's those life matters that lend a hand to opportunities such as this project.

2019, oh how much of a great and challenging year it was (even as it *zoooooomed* by)! Though it was a great and challenging year, it offered many distractions that inadvertently detoured me off course of completing this book in a timely manner.

Yea the End! The End? The End! *The Completion!* Well not a shame to state *I did not make the original date slated for!* Banking on my Father who Blessed me to complete this *14th Masterpiece!* That it will inspire and empower, motivate many great people reading the contents of this book. Surely, they will walk away with a new and rejuvenated outlook on themselves and their purpose.

A definite lesson sits within this journey, as well the stories outlined in this penned book. From the start whatever arrives to take you off course, stay focus regardless of the course you might be distracted from. The vision of your passionate course should never be deleted, even if life causes a delay of that passionate course or path.

To further, there is many who've derailed from their plan path, their passionate path and never recovered. That is not to say those who never recovered where lost to eternity! No, because they must continue to live and construct the daily of this life. We all know, if we miss a beat *"life will beat right on past us!"* So, at the end of the day, be cautious and aware of those monkey wrenches that surely attempt to throw you off your life game plan. That's a real mother for you, not finding your path of life and living it, so stick to it, make it happen *regardless of the circumstances!*

In Retrospect, this moment is now and forever which will direct you through the many avenue's life has to off er. Be prepared at this junction, now that you have completed reading and digesting the contents of this book. Be agile to aspire and conquer the challenges that beckon you. Whether that challenge is disguised as a person, thing, matter, material or other, *"POWER UP"* to overtake the roadblock that is attempting to stop you from *"CONTINUING THE DREAM"* and *"MOVE BY FAITH, AND NOT FEAR!"*

"OH HAPPY DAY" should be the mark set as the final analogy in *"FINDING FAVOR"* for *"THANKS-GIVING"* and knowing you *"WILL OVERCOME!"* It will keep you *"IN WITH THE NEW"* as the signal for *"RING, RING, RING, THE BELL!"* Alert *"WAKE UP, WAKE UP EVERBODY"* you are a *"WINNER"* filled with presence to be *"GREAT"* and far from *"DONE!"*

As I close, I close with these remarks:
"STAY TRUE TO YOUR FAITH AND CONTINUE TO PRESS FORTH! SIDESTEP ANY AND ALL SHADE MOVING TOWARDS YOUR DESTINY! YOUR DESTINY IS THE TRADEMARK OF YOUR LEGACY!!!!"
THE END

Motivational Moments

Interested in DLD earlier *Books & DVDS*?
Order these products online or *Directly* from DLD *Today*
at *Discount Prices* for your reading & viewing pleasure.

TRUTH IN THE POEM
Very First book 1992.
On Sale $5.95

THE KEY:
Second Book 1994
On Sale $5.95

THE NEGRO ALMANAC
Compiled Black History
On Sale $5.95

EXCELLENZE IN
MY HOODZ – 1997
On Sale $9.95

THE POWER OF BEING
A W-I-N-N-E-R – 2013
No. 1 BEST SELLER
On Sale $15.99

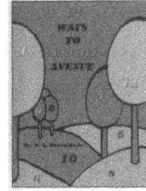
12 WAYS
Published 1998
On Sale $6.95

PROSPERITY
Published 1998
On Sale $6.95

10 REASONS
Published 2004
On Sale $5.95

1ST ANN BLK HERITAGE
Published 2001
On Sale $7.95

T. P. O. B. A W. / DVD
The Seminar – 2014
On Sale $12.95

LIVING HISTORY / DVD
DLD as
"FREDERICK DOUGLASS"
2013 / On Sale $12.95

THE G. U. HOLIDAY
Motivational DVD
On Sale $12.95

All Products Are Copyrighted Material by DLD Enterprises, Washington, D.C. 20010

Motivational Moments

THANK YOU

&

BLESSINGS
AS YOU CONTINUE TO ENJOY

HEALTH – FAMILY – SUCCESS!
PROSPERITY – GREATNESS &
ELEVATION!

Yours Sincerely:
MOTIVATIONAL GURU
DONALD L. DOWRIDGE, JR.

www.ingramcontent.com/pod-product-compliance
Lightning Source LLC
Chambersburg PA
CBHW022119090426
42743CB00008B/925